CW00521709

Kala Jordan-Lindsey

WHEN
YOU
RISE

AN INSPIRATIONAL POEM OF HOPE FOR THE NATION

BOOK 1

When You Rise
Copyright© 2021 by Kala Jordan-Lindsey

Kala Jordan-Lindsey
Published Author
For speaking engagements visit:
www.visiblevoiceohyes.com
KalaL@visiblevoiceohyes.com

Designed & published by
Emphaloz Publishing House
www.emphaloz.com
publish@emphaloz.com

Photo credits: AJ Distique Photography

WHEN YOU RISE

Kala Jordan-Lindsey

at dawn when you rise

open your eyes

look at the sun
listen to hearts beat
and listen to the sounds of beautiful feet

do you hear the uproar across this globe?

we're struggling with spiritual warfare

violence

deaths

weaponization

immigration

poverty

unemployment

and education

while an unprecedented pandemic
continues to affect the nation

many are weak

sick

tired

overwhelmed

frustrated

depressed

lost

and disturbed by the precious lives who
are homeless
poor
mentally ill
and dying on *Skid Row* streets

in New York City and all over the land

hate is escalating

hearts are deteriorating

and innocent lives are being taken

what's going on (in the voice of Marvin
Gaye)?

do you ever wonder if we will rise as one
nation, under God,

with liberty, and justice for all?

or if we will continue to fight, steal, and
kill one another

on a planet where grace binds us all
together?

let's stand like trees

blossom like flowers

sing like birds

and fly like eagles

high in the sky
on purpose
with purpose
and for a greater purpose

striving together
loving together
and growing in Christ together

through ups and downs
no matter the condition
nor the weather

hope sustains us all together

so, let's love each other

in unity
like birds that flock together

let's live in harmony

let's choose to be the change
and be the difference

let's stay hopeful
have faith
gain wisdom
obey
and listen

and forgive before it's too late

don't worry, but pray
and never give up
because blessings are on the way

in the midst of an unprecedented
pandemic

choose life, and love God's way—the
right way

exercise humility

and compassion

when I rise
I hear human beings cry

scream

and shout

at the top of their lungs

I hear voices through homes
businesses
government centers
schools
churches
playgrounds
malls
fairs
amusement parks
restaurants
grocery stores
arenas
institutions
cemeteries
hospitals
and across the Atlantic Ocean

they're mentally
physically
and spiritually ill
many have degrees
and are still jobless
at a standstill

do you care?

do you empathize with other lives?

let's strive together to help each other
overcome life

let's step up and stand out
on purpose
with purpose
and for a greater purpose

millions are hopeless
helpless
and homeless

they're confused about life
as they wonder
whether they
should they give up
or continue to fight

some sit
while others search for life
from daybreak to sunset

while a handful turn to illegal drugs
and alcohol
prostitution
and careless sex

they roam in the streets, and in the
scorching heat

surrounded by tents
with dents
holes
rust
decay
feces
and mold

many are beat
bruised
scolded
and crave
to one day
live rather than just be alive

so at dawn when they rise
they question
what's going on?

why are we losing lives?
why are we suffering?
is there hope, today and tomorrow?

let's encourage one another

and pray for our neighbors

let's be grateful
kind
caring
helpful
humble
meek
patient
loving
giving
compassionate
and careful listeners

many are strong
but weak
because they lack spiritual food
to see

for years
they've slept
and stood
with ordinary faces
endured discrimination
experienced hate
listened to senseless debates
and faced intimidation

all while walking
in bodies
where greatness is asleep

have you seen the buildings, sidewalks,
and the streets?

their unbelievable

I see graffiti

I see men and women
living in tents
sleeping on sidewalks
sitting on buckets
searching in trash cans
and searching for food to eat

don't we all desire to survive and eat?

can you see through my heart?

many live near dumpsters
alleys
tunnels
prisons
and under bridges

and near streets
where the wealthy eat

they're loud
like a million trumpets playing in unison

but their hearts are weak

they're powerless

fragile

depressed

and spiritually blind

they sit in bodies
where greatness is bleak

but there is hope

so, when you rise
count your blessings

and never give up

life is real

and these streets are unbelievably
disturbing
shocking
unbearable
and senseless

yes, many don't rest

but a handful strive to do their best

millions are in a mess

so, how can they save, retire, and invest?

what a nation

can't we see?

I see powerful voices
all around me

but many are imprisoned

in precious bodies
where greatness is bleak

on every street
I see boys and girls
waving
running
skipping
hopping
and playing
with the cutest smiles

some with dimples
some with frowns
some with laughs

with potential
to rise in this small, but big world

when I gaze

I hear the melody of Armstrong's
What a Wonderful World

what a song of special memories
of my sisters and I
as little girls

we wore ponytails and curls
ran
played
and turned in swirls

we jumped on trampolines
sat on swings
laughed
cried
hugged each other
and did other things
with our father
and beautiful mother

life was a wonderful world
but, today, many are going insane

it's unsafe

but we're safe in Jesus Christ

many are losing their minds
and committing suicide

they're on drugs

and addicted to alcohol

they're in the hospital
and millions have died

many have left loved ones behind

crying

while our boys and girls are being
influenced
in this precious world

some are bullied
while others are beat

they're lost
so they live careless each and every day

we think it's okay
but our sons and daughters have so much
to say

like a balloon waiting to explode
on any given day

let's wake up and pay attention

and encourage our loved ones
around the world
to stand up and believe
strive and succeed

soar

and never give up

through every closed
and opened door

there is hope

despite the nation's uproar
where many are crying for hearts to listen
to give
to care
to love
to feed
and instill discipline

so, when you rise

motivate a child
a friend
a loved one

and desire peace

let's communicate
compliment
congratulate
and strive to teach one another

let's look each other in the eyes
and encourage one another to look
forward
stay focused
and rise

because in today's time
people are losing their minds

their drinking and driving
speeding
and acting wild

life is meaningless in their eyes
so it's hard to lift their head, and walk
think
talk
pray
love
give
sing
forgive
and rise

on these streets, I see men with bald heads
fades
long hair
short cuts
and waves

many look for food to eat

they're tired

and they can't breathe

many feel overwhelmed with life
so they carry strife
and stay awake at night

they're lost
lonely
down
upset
angry
fearful
anxious
hopeless

and struggling
in bodies
where greatness is bleak

where there's hope

I hear men and women
on sidewalks
walking down staircases
shouting at train stations
smoking
and drinking their lives away

while many talk about their futures
hopes
dreams
plans
memories
and love

but many are imprisoned
in bodies
where greatness is bleak

at stop lights
I see the homeless
begging for coins
sweating
and shouting for help
without sufficient sleep

while some dance on their feet
near bars
and strip clubs
where many are blessed
with food to eat

do you know who's on these streets?

it's time to open your eyes

at dawn when you rise

I see the greedy
but also the needy
with signs
crying
begging for food
and water

while they struggle
as wives and mothers

they struggle to grind
just to earn a dime
with life on their mind

as brave men and women—husbands and
wives

protect
and embrace
their daughters

while a handful question, how will I
survive without a 9-5
8 to 4
7 to 3
or without money to buy medications
and food to eat?

and while they drive
and stand

they search near trash cans
sidewalks and in the streets
for something to satisfy
their empty stomachs
and minds before they sleep

they watch many do all they can
like an army of lions fighting for its cubs
for the sake of love

what a nation—can't we see?

or are we blind?

stay humble

don't live selfishly

don't desire violence
war
rage
and envy

there's no hope in weapons
no success in hate
and no blessings in lies

but there's hope in the nation's cries

we're on this ship together
where no man can disappear
from earthquakes
unpredictable weather
trials and tribulations
struggles
obstacles
and whatever else life brings

grace is binding us all together

never give up

there's hope for the nation
despite its heart's disorder

an illness

and serious bleed

it's greater than what you and I can see

I'm convinced

but do you believe it?

do you believe
there are many imprisoned
in bodies
where greatness is bleak?

when you rise

open your eyes

look at the adults in cars
while they dance
to loud beats

and look at the actions
as many race on the highways
in the scorching heat

while many exit
the Miami streets
as they bob their heads
snap their fingers
and dance
to *Juju on That Beat*

WHEN YOU RISE

I hear arguing
fussing
and foul language

I see anger

many are hurting
embarrassed
shameful
depressed
lost
blind
and sick of the grind

they're clueless to these signs

because they stand imprisoned
in tents
where greatness is bleak

are you awake?

can you hear?

can you see?

many bodies are imprisoned

where greatness is bleak

when I walk down the street
I see the rich
and the poor
where buildings are high
like the sky
luxurious
gated
lit
wide
and perfect-looking—on the outside

but on the inside
I see bodies
where greatness is bleak

so, at dawn when you rise

open your eyes

be thankful

have faith

be hopeful

shine like stars
walk by faith
live with happiness
breathe with joy
sing with confidence
dance with boldness
and love on purpose

pray

meditate

dream

embrace today
and be patient for tomorrow

live, laugh, and love
and give every day your best
as if today was your last

be strong

be the change

be the difference

let God open your eyes and soften your
hearts

be grateful and stay hopeful

when you rise

You are Ever Special!

Kala Jordan-Lindsey
Published Author
For speaking engagements visit:
www.visiblevoiceohyes.com
KalaL@visiblevoiceohyes.com

Thank You and God Bless

Kala Jordan-Lindsey is a poet and published author of the decade. Her works have attracted thousands around the world and continue to inspire her readers. Her second book, *Words from the Heart,* is a collection of poetry and prose and was an instant bestseller and five-star favorite by many readers. Kala is currently working on *Words from the Heart: Young Readers' Edition, She,* a fiction prose series, *A Heart*

of Gratitude, a 12-Day Devotional, *Jordan and the Spelling Bee,* a children's book, *The Person Behind the Clarinet,* a Memoir, and many more. She currently resides in Miami, Florida, with her spouse and their beautiful daughter, and says, *Writing is an environment worth experiencing like no other where living, breathing, releasing, and tasting freedom is certainly a blessing and privilege.*

-Kala

Lightning Source UK Ltd.
Milton Keynes UK
UKHW051444290821
389335UK00012B/17